ELETED

W9-BZU-968

WHAT HAPPENED TO THE
DINOSAURS?

by Franklyn M. Branley   illustrated by Marc Simont

Thomas Y. Crowell   New York

11004767

Other Recent Let's-Read-and-Find-Out Science Books® You Will Enjoy

Shooting Stars • My Five Senses • A Drop of Blood • Switch On, Switch Off • The Skeleton Inside You • Feel the Wind • Ducks Don't Get Wet • Tornado Alert • Digging Up Dinosaurs • The Beginning of the Earth • Eclipse • The Sun: Our Nearest Star • Dinosaur Bones • Glaciers • Snakes Are Hunters • Danger—Icebergs! • Comets • Evolution • Rockets and Satellites • The Planets in Our Solar System • The Moon Seems to Change • Ant Cities • Get Ready for Robots! • Gravity Is a Mystery • Snow Is Falling • Journey into a Black Hole • What Makes Day and Night • Air Is All Around You • Turtle Talk • What the Moon Is Like • Hurricane Watch • Sunshine Makes the Seasons • My Visit to the Dinosaurs • The BASIC Book • Bits and Bytes • Germs Make Me Sick! • Flash, Crash, Rumble, and Roll • Volcanoes • Dinosaurs Are Different • What Happens to a Hamburger • Meet the Computer • How to Talk to Your Computer • Rock Collecting • Is There Life in Outer Space? • All Kinds of Feet • Flying Giants of Long Ago • Rain and Hail • Why I Cough, Sneeze, Shiver, Hiccup, & Yawn • You Can't Make a Move Without Your Muscles • The Sky Is Full of Stars • No Measles, No Mumps for Me

The *Let's-Read-and-Find-Out Science Book* series was originated by Dr. Franklyn M. Branley, Astronomer Emeritus and former Chairman of the American Museum–Hayden Planetarium, and was formerly co-edited by him and Dr. Roma Gans, Professor Emeritus of Childhood Education, Teachers College, Columbia University. For a complete catalog of Let's-Read-and-Find-Out Science Books, write to Thomas Y. Crowell Junior Books, Harper & Row, Publishers, Inc., 10 East 53rd Street, New York, NY 10022.

Let's-Read-and-Find-Out Science Book is a registered trademark of Harper & Row, Publishers, Inc.

What Happened to the Dinosaurs?
Text copyright © 1989 by Franklyn M. Branley
Illustrations copyright © 1989 by Marc Simont
All rights reserved. No part of this book may be used or reproduced in any manner whatsoever without written permission except in the case of brief quotations embodied in critical articles and reviews. Printed in the United States of America. For information address Thomas Y. Crowell Junior Books, 10 East 53rd Street, New York, N.Y. 10022.
10 9 8 7 6 5 4 3 2 1

First Edition

Library of Congress Cataloging-in-Publication Data
Branley, Franklyn Mansfield, 1915–
    What happened to the dinosaurs?

    (A Let's-read-and-find-out science book)
    Summary: Describes various scientific theories which explore the extinction of the dinosaurs.
    1. Dinosaurs—Juvenile literature. 2. Extinction (Biology)—Juvenile literature. [1. Dinosaurs.
2. Extinction (Biology)] I. Simont, Marc, ill. II. Title.
III. Series.
QE862.D5B66 1989   567.9′1   88-37626
ISBN 0-690-04747-9
ISBN 0-690-04749-5 (lib. bdg.)

WHAT HAPPENED TO THE
DINOSAURS?

What happened to the dinosaurs?

5

Dinosaurs lived on Earth for 140 million years. Then, 65 million years ago, they disappeared. Other reptiles disappeared, too—flying reptiles and reptiles that lived in the sea. Many other kinds of animals also died out. And many kinds of plants.

No one knows why the dinosaurs disappeared.

But there are many theories. A theory is an idea.

It is an explanation that might be possible.

Maybe small animals ate dinosaur eggs so only

a few eggs were able to hatch. This is one theory. But this theory does not explain why other kinds of animals died out, and many plants as well. Also, some dinosaurs may not have laid eggs.

Maybe a group of dinosaurs got sick and the sickness spread to other groups. That's possible, for even today diseases spread among herds of cattle. But if that happened, chances are the sickness would not have reached reptiles that lived in the sea. Also, other kinds of animals would not have caught the sickness, and neither would plants.

Some people have suggested that for a time the sun became cooler and did not shine as brightly. That made Earth cooler, so plants could not grow well. Some dinosaurs were meat eaters—they ate other dinosaurs. But many dinosaurs ate plants. They needed a lot of food. If Earth cooled so much the plants could not grow, plant-eating and meat-eating dinosaurs would have starved.

These are some theories to explain what happened to the dinosaurs.

Another theory was suggested by scientists who were exploring old layers of rocks. In rock layers 65 million years old they found dinosaur fossils. They also found iridium. That's a rare metal, most of which is deep inside the Earth. And they found a layer of black soot, or carbon, that might have been produced by a great fire.

Traces of iridium have been found in meteorites that have fallen to Earth. And scientists believe that the metal may be found in comets, too. Sixty-five million years ago thousands of comets may have crashed into Earth. That would have produced a lot of heat. Wildfires would have swept through forests and swamps. Plants would have burned up, and dinosaurs would have, too. Only small animals that could dig into the ground would have escaped.

After the fire had burned out, the theory says, the air was heavy with soot, ash, and dust. There was so much, the sun could not shine through. Earth got colder and colder. Many plants that had survived the fire could not grow. There was little food for any dinosaurs that might have survived the Earth fire. So they starved.

The dust cloud may have hung over Earth for several months or even a year. Gradually it settled, making the layers of iridium and soot that scientists have discovered.

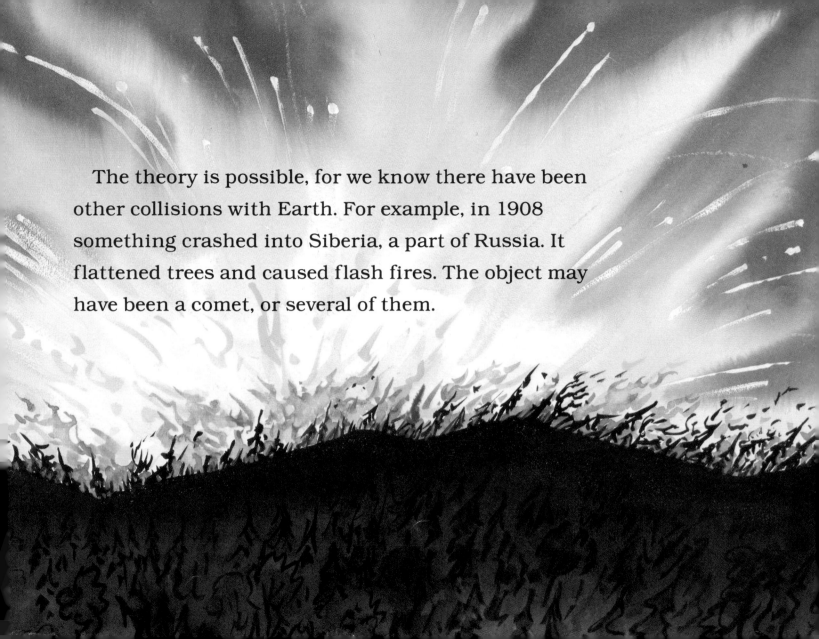

The theory is possible, for we know there have been other collisions with Earth. For example, in 1908 something crashed into Siberia, a part of Russia. It flattened trees and caused flash fires. The object may have been a comet, or several of them.

Every 26 to 30 million years showers of comets may hit Earth. That's what some scientists think. They study fossils in very old layers of rock and in newer layers, too. They think they see signs that every 26 to 30 million years, different kinds of animals and plants have died out.

But, they wonder, why should the comet showers occur every 26 to 30 million years? Why should they happen so regularly? Some people answer the question this way: They say that the sun has a twin. The two stars move around one another, and it takes about 26 million years for them to go around once. No one has found such a star, but it has been named. It is called the Nemesis star. ("Nemesis" means "trouble." When the dinosaurs met their nemesis, they were in trouble.)

Way out beyond the solar system, we know, there is a huge cloud of dust. Comets come from this cloud.

Maybe every 26 million years the Nemesis star comes in closer to the cloud and pulls dust out of it. The dust collects together, making clusters of comets. The comets race through space, most of them becoming space wanderers. But many collide with our planet. If this theory is correct, there will be comet collisions in the future. The theory says that the next one will be about 13 million years from now.

We know *what* happened to the dinosaurs. They disappeared. But we do not know why. We only have theories.

Maybe the correct answer is in one of these different theories. Maybe, as many believe, there really was a tremendous comet collision, and wild Earth fire. Dust and ash may have darkened the skies and blocked out the sun. Maybe there is a Nemesis star that passes near the dust cloud every 26 million years.

No one knows. But we can be sure that scientists will keep trying to find out which theory is the right one.

Why the dinosaurs disappeared is still a mystery.